HOW TO MAKE YOUR BUSINESS #1 IN YOUR INDUSTRY WITHIN 90 DAYS OR LESS

Mike Pantouvakis

DEDICATION

This book is fully dedicated to you, the reader.
This is my way of saying thank you for getting
one step closer to achieving your full potential
and beginning this mythical journey to the
promised land!

CONTENTS

ACKNOWLEDGMENTS

I want to acknowledge all the immensely successful people who donated their time to me and taught me what I know try to teach to others. I will not name names, because that could be a book on its own, but without their help none of this would ever be possible. Thank you for sharing your wisdom with me and guiding me to the right direction of unfathomable, unstoppable success. I am forever in your debt.

OVERVIEW

After reading this booklet you will have learned how to effectively transform your business to a money-making machine like no other, while also staying at the top of your industry. I will not only share with you secrets the top 0.001% of business owners have shared with me, but also the knowledge $150,000 of self-investment has given while also sharing what one of the top schools of business in the country teaches thoroughly. So, **pay close attention**. All I am asking of you is if you truly find that this material can add significant value to your business and you feel that you need someone who is an expert to guide you through the process, while you get to focus on what matters most to your business, *schedule an appointment* with one of our representatives and let us *guide you* through the process. Now that that's out of the way, here's an outline of what I'll cover in the following pages.

First, we're going to talk a little bit about how the natural tendencies of the business cycle is to eliminate you in the long run. After all, only 4% of business survive after 10 years, and "survive" does not mean make profit. A lot fewer than 4% make profit. Trust me, **if you don't have the right strategies and technologies in place you will die in the business battlefield.**

Then, we will cover a little bit about the basic concept of cognitive bias and perceptual filters. This is one of the most fundamental mistakes business owners make when managing their business. And the worst part? 100% of them when asked what is wrong will respond "I just don't know", and that is only because it's by definition unconscious behavior. **If you can spot it, you can win it**, and *I'll show you how to do that.*

After that, I'll demonstrate to you why and how exactly technology and innovation is vital to you and your business. **The most common mistake is not the lack of innovation in times of war, it is the lack of innovation in times of peace.** So, we'll dive into how you can make the most out of the technology that's accessible today and how you can be ready for next technological movements that are coming *very, very soon.*

Finally, we are going to examine the most important part of running a business: the stunningly intuitive formula that will guide you through when the waters are calm but also help you **thrive** acting as your *guiding light when the waters are trying to sink you in.* This is a very common-sense formula, but we'll dive in just the right depth so that you can use it and stay on top during every economic season

THE NATURAL BUSINESS CYCLE:
96% OF BUSINESSES FAIL WITHIN 10 YEARS.

I t is no *secret* that *business vibrates risk*, because we *never really know* what will happen and what will actually make the markets move up or down and if we will be ever *necessary again*, but since you are reading this I'm assuming you are one of the very few who actually decided to take matters into their own hands and aspire to **create a life that you want.** However, it is definitely worth acknowledging the reasons that most business fail. If while you are reading them find some that resonate with you, **you need to take action to change that, because it will**

destroy you in the long run.

According to a study done by Forbes on October of 2018 there are *specific reasons* for the fall of businesses worldwide. First reason is "no market need". At some point every business solves a problem, and that problem might be very "hot" for a while, providing cashflow to the business. This, however, history has shown is immensely prone to change and the more businesses let external factors pass by, the more the actual business suffers. Let me give you an example so *I can paint the picture in your head better.* Back in the late 19th century cars had just started being introduced to the marketplace. Some of the highest valued companies at the time were companies that made horse carriages. They made the carriages and sold them to whoever needed them, and they made a LOT of money... Then in 1896 the first car is introduced to the roads. But it wasn't that simple for the horse carriage companies. They laughed at the idea of the four-wheel mobile. They treated it like a **joke**. They had both the **capital and the personnel** need to build a competing car. They stuck to carriages... Can you imagine how different the world would look if they had seen the trend and adapted to the future needs? Your new Tesla might have been competing against 200 years of experienced manufacturers. It's not. Oh, and by the way can you guess *why* they didn't spot the evolution? Because **their pockets were full, and their eyes were fixated** on what was in their minds instead of what demand was out there in the future... It is human nature to get stuck in your own bubble of thought. This is why it's a great idea sometimes to *consult with a friend who knows what the hell they're talking about.* Anyway, my point is they didn't adapt to the future and they **died!**

Just like this example there are billions happening every day the slowly but surely compound into an unfortunate cancer that is destroying businesses and giving birth to new smarter ones. The only way to stay in the game is to be able to tell what the demand of the **future** is. I'm going to tell you an obvious thing that every single one of the 96/100 of the failing business owners and managers get wrong. This is truly a recipe for long-term success if you know how to apply it to your business, and if you only get this from me, you are going to rise your sales and biz lifetime by 25%-150% approximately. See, the carriage people missed something fundamental. They missed the fact that they were **not** in the carriage business, they were in the **transportation** business. It's obvious now, but Ford new that transportation was timeless, so he made the car, **they didn't**. *That's the magic.*

While this is great and we can all get really excited now, there have been multiple examples of managers of MASSIVE business that have misinterpreted that miserably. We are talking about giants of industries, Ivy league alumni, and self-made billionaires. Yeah, if they can get it wrong **so can you**... Don't get *me* wrong

7

though, you might very well be either one of the above or have *perfect mental capacity* to evaluate situations and be in a position to *make the best decisions for you and your business.* What every single case of those I have personally studied, and my team has thoroughly reviewed, is that they never *seek for advice!* And it is absolutely understandable that people are emotional beings and they can sometimes make **irrational decisions** when they know how much **they stand to lose**. More on this on later chapters though.

So yeah, this is a potentially painful reality to some, but **when embraced can make all the difference** between the person you read about on the Forbes billionaire list and the guy who lost all of his money, his family savings, his wife left him etc... You get the point. On to chapter number two!

THE CANCER OF BUSINESS: WHAT IS THE REAL INVISIBLE FORCE THAT IS KILLING YOUR BUSINESS?

You see, any good neurologist knows that the mere hyper-complexity of the world we live in would totally overload our brains to the point where they couldn't function, unless there were certain technologies that our brains have developed over **millions of years** of evolution that **keep us safe**. Once you become aware of these natural phenomena, you'll not only be able to spot them in yourself, but they will also *become evident* to you when they occur in *other people*.

So, what exactly am I talking about? You see, our minds evolved to the point where in order for them to make sense of everything going on in the world around us, they focus on **specific things**. Let me give you an example. Some time ago I met this gorgeous girl and every time she looked at me, I thought to myself "Oh wow, I'm so lucky to have her" and my heart would instantaneously melt of joy. So, from this point onward I went on with life and *everything that happened to me made me feel I was lucky*... Regardless of whether I was or not everything **seemed** that way to me... I could be in a serious car accident and I would thankful to my *lady luck* that nothing **worse** happened to me, instead of **blaming god** that I didn't deserve to be at that time at that place. And guess what, after some time my friends started to *see* this luck I had acquired. You might have had a similar experience, or you might have seen it in your friends and loved ones that they **acquired a similar attribute after an event in their lives**. Now, there are two sides to every coin. I have met, and listened to, many, many business owners offer what they think is the best product in their market, **but their customers just don't seem to agree.** They always blame "trolls" and "haters" for their declining revenues and bad reputation. They are **fully convinced**, and if they talk to you long enough, you just might be *hypnotized* in believing actually have the best product! As soon as they walk out that door, though, you get to *truly evaluate* their product and find the **common truth**! Notice the pattern here?

See, my examples are only to illustrate to you that this phenomenon can act either for you or against you. In the language of neuroscience these are called *perceptual filters* and they alter our perception of reality in such a way that reinforce the current state of mind we're in. That's why I'm guessing that you have had an argument with someone and then resolved it, and then everything you said for the next 20 minutes or so just **pissed them off.** In behavioral economics the same thing on a different level is called cognitive bias. *You get the idea...* The point is if you are not aware of **it will crush you and your business to the ground!**

Let me tell you a story about a friend I had a

11

while back named Marcus. Marcus was a *good friend of mine,* good guy. I've known Marcus since high school and we're still very close. One day, I look at my phone and what do I see? It's my buddy Marcus calling me! I pick up the phone and I listen to him ecstatically outlining to me his new business pursuit. He told me all about it. How it was going to be the **best transportation company** the world has ever seen, how it was going to offer the best prices for better quality rides... You know, he told me everything. I genuinely was really excited for my friend, but I told him with simple words "Marcus, *you are my good friend,* and I think if you put your best into the business it will manage to keep up with your expectations of it, but as of right now your business plan has 1000 loopholes that are so *obvious to me*, that if not looked at **will murder you in the business battlefield...**" He thanked me, hang up, and for 3 months I didn't hear from him... Then, he texts me with a heartwarming message saying that he is ready to listen now after he lost the first round! He told me "Mike, I want you to know that **I am ready to listen**, because some things that you *advised me about from the very beginning,* I was **completely oblivious** to... I wonder *how much better* my business would be *if only I listened to you before I started...*"

You see, Marcus mind was not allowing him to **truly see**. He simply didn't **know better**, and so *he paid for it with his money and with the stress and chaos he caused to himself and to his loved ones.* Instead, if only he listened to his friend and not be a slave to his cognitive biases and perceptual filters, he would have *easily levitated over the tremendously stressful pain of losing* and would have *ripped all the incredible rewards that come from a truly heroic victory.* Now, that is not to say that you will **never** have casualties, even with the best advisor at your side, but you **certainly** will be *more likely* to keep those to the bear minimum while marching towards the so glorious path of seeing your

13

business *succeed and thrive beyond your imagination.*

So, what can you do to really be the one controlling your mind in a way that genuinely allows you to beat the odds and have your mind **work for you** instead of against you? It's simple, in order to program the machine, you have to know what you want the machine to do. So how do you practically do that? To begin with, having a clear vision of where your business eventually needs to go and feeling how good that would make you feel, will put you in a particular winning mindset. While a lot of people will say **that** will help you on its own, I say it will trigger your perceptual filters so that instead of looking to reinforce stupid ideas that don't work, find you solutions that you **might have missed** if you were not in that state. I told you this mechanism *can work for you* or against you! What else can you do? Well, you can take a look at your history of decision making, find out when exactly you made a decision from a stupid state of mind, *see the impact* that caused, imagine how the outcome would be different if you were in a better state of mind, then make a forecast of upcoming similar decisions, and then try to *use your intuition* to predict similar situations so that your logical thinking will dictate when you get in a good state of mind, so that you *maximize your profits.* Finally, what you can do if you don't want to endure the pain of having to learn all the aforementioned is you can simply **ask for consultation.** *See, me* and my team can offer up to 15 minutes of free consultation to most people, so even if you're starting out you can get on the line with us, give some basic info, and be on the way to driving your business to the next level with all the new, innovative, and intuitive things you are going to learn. As an upside to this if you *like our advice,* we can make it come to life and go into tremendous length to make sure you get what was promised, *you hire us* that is. Having said that, it doesn't even have to be **Skyline Consulting** *you get the advice from,* you can find

15

any advisor that you **feel suits your needs and wants** in a way that truthfully **adds value** to your business and have them cross check you.

So yeah, now you already belong to the top 0.1% of business owners I would guess, since most owners don't truly go to lengths to find out about the **science of improving performance** in the business world. I will tell you though, out of those who do, 0.01% of them know about the massive technological movements that will literally make the difference between a **dying business** full of problems and a **thriving business** full of eager to expand and create more opportunities. So, what are you waiting for, go to the next chapter and start learning about this!

YOU ADAPT OR YOU DIE: "THE MEASURE OF INTELLIGENCE IS THE ABILITY TO CHANGE."

Have you ever wondered why multi-billion corporations that have ruled for decades, even centuries, go bankrupt and bend in front of the world humiliated? Well, it's not really that complex. Blockbuster was the go-to store for movie rentals. The company was making **unbelievably large amounts** of money. Literally, they had the crushing majority of the market of movie rentals, the entire US was in love with it. Then, a small startup came up called Netflix. I'm assuming you have heard of that name. Netflix offered a subscription-based service where they would ship you all the DVD's. Then they moved to online streaming and that's when Blockbuster *laughed*. And I mean why wouldn't they? They were in the market for decades and they **KNEW** for a fact that the movie rental industry isn't going to change. I mean it would be insane for people to go on their computer and rent movies from there! Billion-dollar industry... If they adapted just 1/100 of their business model to get into Netflix competition, you and I would be talking about how the new season of Game of Thrones is coming to Blockbuster... Why? Well I'll let Blockbuster CEO Jim Keyes explain with his own words: "Neither Redbox nor Netflix are even on the radar screen in terms of competition, it's more Wal-Mart and Apple". He said that in 2008. Two years later, in 2010, his company filed for bankruptcy. Netflix as of 2019 is worth over 150 Billion USD. With a "B".

I'm making you aware of this case study to remind you that **it is not in the times of war that will kill you, it is in times of perceived**

peace where you are convinced you the world is headed the way you want it. It's *simple* really, isn't it? Keyes couldn't see that he was being attacked by Netflix, because *things were going great.* Let me let you in on a little secret. The fundamental fabric of business is built upon the idea that the best business prevails. Now, since there is a benefit to starting a new business - money, improving the world, love for the game, ***money*** - businesses will always keep being created. And since they will always keep being created, if you don't **constantly adapt**, you **will** die miserably. This is what happened to a billion-dollar company, with tens of millions of users, and Ivy league graduates on the managerial positions... It can happen to you too, *you know*. Don't be sad though, I made a promise to *assist* you in making your business *great* and I **will live up to my word**.

So how do you adapt in a way that constantly beats all of your opposition? See, most people reading that would think "Ahh... I don't want to change already, let me go home watch some TV. This game you're playing is pointless and exhausting, you are never *going to win*..." Yes, this is *most* people, but since you are reading this, you are not most people... Chances are that at the notion that there could be a way that *I will show you* right now to consistently beat everyone else and have your business win over customers and **take over cities**, your hands start to sweat slightly, your breathing shortens and *gets excited* while it waits, and your heart beats a little faster than before... Now, that's more like a good attitude! So, what's the right answer? Well, let me introduce you to the world of social media marketing...

You see, whether you are familiar with that space or not, the single greatest marketing asset your business will ever have is a good social media campaign (and obviously *campaign manager*). A long time ago people used to live inside their newspapers, so naturally the ads on the paper made the most money *for the advertisers*, because they had the **most eyes**. Yet, they were **severely expensive** for something without guarantees. Then came the radio, and again all ears were on the radio, *until they weren't*. Then the TV, that lasted a tad longer, but now even super bowl ads can't make a lot of money for the *people who pay a fortune* to put them there... This is because a new medium came into our lives, that extremely few people know how to use to **generate revenues**, yet if that medium was a country it would be the **largest country** in the world *today*... Social media is where the world is going, and we are *already late* to adapt to it... Let me tell you a little about how this field works, having studied it for over 7 years now and having created businesses *out of thin air* with it...

Advertising on most other media in the history of the world has been **radically impersonal** and it has been based on the principle that "You pay us a lot of money, we show your ad to a lot of people, and you **might** make some sales..." Yet, Facebook and the other online platforms appear to work in a vastly *different manner*. You see, Facebook's ad campaigns work like this "You pay us *pennies on the dollar* every time we make **sure** someone sees/clicks/ engages with your ad". See, it really doesn't matter if you have the best product in the world, *if no one knows it exists*, **no one is going to buy it.** This is *really why* **social media marketing is the future**.

So, let me give you some *free* advice that will return massive value to your business. As a business owner to another, if you are not getting as many sales as you would like, get your marking executives or whoever is responsible for doing your marketing, to **stop** being involved in social media... This is truly a **beatable game!** All the social media we use are meant to be addictive, that means that users are going to be spending a lot of time in this medium; 2.27 billion people use Facebook at least once a month... So why would you want

them to **not** be involved in what I just *proved* to
you is the future? Simple! See, while social
media can be a platform where your business is
shown to the world, and the world celebrates it,
the **wrong kind** of advertisement can act as a
force that slowly, but *surely* **kills** your precious
business. Now, if your management team is
good, and I don't doubt it is amazing, you will
be able to get over the bad reputation if you
prove to the world that you are worth forgiving.
Think about it, one simple harmless mistake can
put you in jeopardy of being **publicly shamed**
for no real reason...

So, you might be thinking "Ok Mike, I get it.
A mistake in social media can hurt me and my
immediate team needs to be kept away from
managing this powerful tool. So, what **do** I
do?". It's true, sometimes the solutions come
from the most obvious places, and you
probably know what I'm about to say... **HIRE
SOMEONE TRULY SKILLED!** Please, I
have seen this mistake happen over and over,

don't let it deteriorate your business. If you *really want to kill your business* there other more honorable ways to go down... Oh by the way, I made a *promise* that I wanted to make your business the **best** version of it, it can ever be and I will *live up to it*. Just to be fully clear, you don't **have** to hire me and my team to manage your social media. However, I really see no reason as to why you wouldn't since you truly have begun to realize that for an advisor to help you *be great,* he needs to *be genuine* in his holistic knowledge of business. I personally think that me and my team have such a basis to be able to help you 10x even 50x your sales, and we'll work with you like you're our only client no matter how busy we are, while we make sure to *deliver* on our promise. As a plus to that, the price you'll pay will always be a tiny, tiny fraction of the *true* value we provide you. Now, if you're *thinking about it* go to https://app.acuityscheduling.com/schedule.php ?owner=18229448 and check for more. Yet, my

24

point was that you don't even need to **hire us**! You can easily google: "social media agency [your location]" and see for the best option...

Now let me tell you a quick story about my friend Dimitris that I think will fully demonstrate my point about how social media can **work for you or against you**... You see, Dimitris had started a small, yet successful apparel brand. He was doing really well selling the accessories his brand had mouth to mouth being the great salesman *he was*... Yet, he lacked a *true* social media presence. I mean, sure he had a couple of posts here and there and maybe a few people saw those, but he didn't have almost any **conversions** from his online store and media... What a *shame* that is if you think about it, such a great salesman that could take something ordinary and present it as if it is diamonds and people are *willing to buy it,* and he couldn't get the *world's biggest forum* and turn thousands, if not hundreds of thousands of people to invest in his luxury accessories... By

this point Dimitris had a really solid foundation
for his brand, he was selling to stores and
boutiques, so he had a great team helping him.
And sure, he was doing good, but something
deep inside his heart new that he could **do better**.
So, what did Dimitris do? He asked his
marketing team to come up with a plan for
advertising on social media to reach more and
more customers. Great idea! So, the team got
their little yellow notepads and started
scribbling strategies that Dimitris would like.
They spent day and night creating this new plan.
There was one problem though, none of them
were qualified to actually take action and get on
with the plan. The great colleges they went to,
which I'm sure you know of them, had not
prepared them adequately to be faced with the
utter jungle of social media. They were
overwhelmed! So, they did what every
unknowledgeable person does in the time of
crisis, they fu**ed up big time. They created a
campaign that was **just terrible**. There were no

calls-to-action, no visual output, no engaging content people would want to share, the targeting was truly more off than you can imagine... And most importantly, being formally "educated" for so many years, they had this grand idea that you have to put a lot of money and then you cross your fingers hoping that what you did worked... Such a stupid thought process! The reality is, you put a little money down and you test! *If the results are good, you put more.* If they are bad you kill it. It's *simple*! People never *come to me first...* All of this could have easily been avoided. Point is Dimitris lost so much money in advertising, you really don't want to know the *stress* he endured the following days, weeks, and months knowing that **all that he had built** from **nothing** could turn to ashes and his empire **removed from the map for good**... However, despite his team being absolute incompetent "know-it-alls", as I said earlier Dimitris was a smart man. *He came to me asking for help...* I took a single look at his strategy and I was convinced that his team should not now, **not ever** interfere with his social media campaigns... I killed some major points, introduced some others, implemented some advanced techniques that are mathematically almost guaranteed to work, and we were good to go. His *luck* turned around exactly *a week after* we implemented the strategies. Facebook's algorithm picked up on the buyers and we were on the way. In total we only spent $140 in ad costs to fix, clear, target, test, and create the entire new strategy, and then it started to *pay* back **MASSIVELY.** Fast forward a couple of weeks down the line, Dimitris had found his peace of mind, feeling more excited to be in the luxury space than ever seeing firsthand how positively the public reacted to his products. Not to mention that he was quite handsomely rewarded, **he made more money in the following weeks than he had made the past couple of years of operations...**

You see, this all became possible through the power of an *algorithmic approach* to what appears *to* be *chaos*. It's only when you apply this **mathematic precision** that you *begin to explore* the utter potential that is **lying on your feet**. Yet, the reason most people fail to truly go there, is because of the fear they have in the entire thing failing. And of course if you pick the wrong team you are bound to make mistakes like the one Dimitris' marketing team made, but on the other hand, if you find the right team I can't even begin to describe to you the benefits you are bound to enjoy with those immediately testable strategies that would take me 1000 pages to write and I still wouldn't have covered 0.000000001% of the subject matter. So, if you care to learn more about that go https://app.acuityscheduling.com/schedule.php ?owner=18229448 and I guarantee you will genuinely be pleasantly surprised by our methodic way of handling randomness

THE PROMISED LAND: "PHYSICS CHANGE, BUT REALITY STAYS THE SAME"

So, you read your way down to right here. I wish I could give you an award for staying with me so long, you really deserve it. Maybe I will... Hopefully you read the quote and you realize that it is not reality that changes, it is our interpretation of it... Now, what does that have to do with anything? See, the point in me showing you this is that I will reveal to you, in just a few moments, the formula that **will** be your map to success. The thing is, before I show you, I want you to be fully aware that this will work for you and your business, but if you don't answer the truth it **will** fail you. Also, this is something most consultants make millions a year keeping secret, so I would ask you to be very careful on who

you show this to, because it is something that **is
powerful.** Finally, I want you to know that
alone we go so far, we humans, are meant to be
together. That's why there is not a single
company that is a one-man job... Alone, you
might be able to survive; in the **right** team, you are
guaranteed to thrive. So, having said all this,
know that there are two ways to implement
what I'll show you. One way is to go about it
the hard way, implement all the steps, manage
your own team, run the risk of completely
crushing your business, because of your inability
to *make the right choice.* Or, alternatively, you
could   go
https://app.acuityscheduling.com/schedule.php
?owner=18229448 and schedule a call, having
all the answers to the questions listed below,
and have a representative, or even me, give the
honesty you have the right to and work with
you to help you make the most of your
business, sharing an insight into the world of
business like no other, that if applied is

31

guaranteed to make you succeed
https://app.acuityscheduling.com/schedule.php
?owner=18229448]. So final thing and I *promise*
I'll show you, while reading from now on,
imagine of your business in every example and
try to think of where you think there is
unexplored potential and what you could do to
improve. I would *advise* you to right down your
answers, questions, concerns and after your
done go here so that we can talk in person too
https://app.acuityscheduling.com/schedule.php
?owner=18229448. So, let's get right to it, after
all I *promised* to show you... The Consumer
Value Journey *has just begun...*

Step 1: Awareness

Ok so let's dive straight into it... Step one, as
you can see is awareness. What does this mean
to your business though? It's simple! The
question here is what are you doing so that
people know you. See, the key here is that for

every sale you make, the first step is always making sure that people **know** who you are. A great misconception that I see all the time is that businesses *think* people buy from who they like. While this isn't false, it's **inaccurate.** The truth is: **People don't buy from who they like, they buy from who they know!** Therefore, it is imperative for your business to absolutely make sure people know you first. I once knew Arianna, she was loved by everyone in her community and everyone respected her dearly, not to mention she was a *great athlete herself.* She had a business that sold specific track and field equipment. She never made a sale until she *asked me what to do.* Her equipment was excellent, a pure product of love for her sport and community, everyone who was involved in track in field loved her and had heard of her endless achievements. So, what went wrong? I asked her a simple question: "Do you let people know about your business or do you naturally expect them to buy from you?". You could see

33

the *enlightenment* in her face when I asked her that... Something so simple it never crossed her mind. Likewise, on a bigger level many businesses need to reach out to their target audience so that they are at least the most known in that community. So do enough people know your brand yet? If they do, do you keep reminding them that you exist, or do you let the competition take your place? Also how do you get to do the best "know" campaign? Would you appreciate some help from a friend who is great at making you known to the people within your exact target audience through social media (https://app.acuityscheduling.com/schedule.php?owner=18229448)? Anyways, you get the point... Knowing is the first out of 7 steps your customers will take going through their journey.

Step 2: Engagement

So now that your customers know you, what

34

do you do to get them *excited about your service* or product? You see, *engaging* someone doesn't mean making a sale, it just means that now that they know who you are and they are having an initial interest in your product/ *service*. Now, think of how many times you, as a consumer, saw something that you though it could potentially be useful in your life or you thought a company's message was really speaking to you. Let me give you yet another example. I was once scrolling through Facebook and I saw some guy talking about some things that I thought were pretty accurate, and I wanted to learn from him. So I clicked on his ad, and I went to his site, and I started reading, and researching if I should buy what he was offering. I was in the *thinking about it* phase. I was intrigued by the things I saw, I was now engaged and involved in the learning of what he was offering. Think about a *sky*scraper. You see the majestic beauty of it, piercing though the clouds 60-70 floors high, yet without its underground base all would collapse, and the top would have never been possible. Step 2 is the base to the *sky*scraper we're trying to build here. How can you make your audience have this initial interaction with your brand? What campaigns would you need to run? How should your website/landing page be structured so that you get people instantly hooked? What technologies would you use to make the most out of the first interactions? Would you think about hiring someone who is an expert in getting initial attention and then directing on to step 3? The point here being that you **need** their attention in order for you to be able to redirect them onto the next step. *Every step is just a steppingstone for the next one*, remember that.

Step 3: Subscribe

Now, we are getting into interesting territory... In this step the customer is passed the *thinking about it* phase and they are actively thinking of spending their precious money to buy what you are offering. They like what you have, or even better *they need it,* and now it's up to you to guide them, just like you would a child learning to navigate through the world, to the final "buy now" button. This step is crucial, merely because it's literally the defining moment where you can either *close the sale* or not. Think about it, how many times have you seen something you liked, done some research on it and found yourself hooked on that something, *craving to give your money in exchange for what the other party is offering.* This is ideally what your customer should be feeling before you make the sale. Now, in truth the more you go through these steps, the more you will realize that a small percentage of people make it to the next step every time. Therefore, your goal is not to get everyone, because that is not only unrealistic, but also because that would hurt the quality of your clients. You see, your goal is to

37

ultimately raise the percentage of great clients that come through your door. Ask yourself, how can you transmit that feeling *you* have felt as a customer to *your customers?* How would you need to present your product/service? How would you need to innovate your product to give them what they really want? How do you innovate your product to give them what they will want in the future? How do you know what they want in the first place? If you have something that's great, where do you find help to get people subscribed to your ideas? Point here is that people *buy feelings* so it would be wise to know what you are really selling. You can always call your friends at skyline consulting for more on this (https://app.acuityscheduling.com/schedule.php?owner=18229448)...

Step 4: Convert

Ahhh... One of my absolute favorite steps in

this journey we have decided to explore. This is where the *sale actually happens*, a fairly self-evident step. However simple it may sound, it is one of the most crucial parts of the process. I want you to try to remember a time where you were relaxed, going about life, and you noticed a brand that you had not heard of before. Then, for something drove you to *decide* to take a better look and you *found yourself* learning more about that service or product and while you were going on at some point something inside of you *just clicked* without a warning, without knowing exactly when, or even how, and *you decided* to **buy** whatever that thing was. This *click* and then the action to *make the purchase* is what converting is all about. Knowing what makes up a good conversion is the key to recreating it. Now, I won't go into depth about exactly what makes up for the highest percentages of conversions, simply because it is a very long topic that needs to be fitted to your specific situation more often than not. All I will say on the subject matter is that while "herd mentality", scarcity, time pressure, are great closing tactics there is much more to making a meaningful sale than those strategies. The most important thing is **offering the right product to the right people**, and after that comes presenting it in a way that appeals to the deepest, wisest part of the brain - the amygdala or otherwise known as the reptilian brain. However, here are some questions that will *guide you* through the process successfully. What did it take for you to be convinced to make the final step? How can you replicate that feeling? Are you targeting the right people who actually will get past this step or are you letting your beliefs stay in the way? Is your product actually going to improve your customer's life? Are the people who give you their money going to get value back from what you're offering 10 times more than what they paid for? If your product is actually going to improve your customers' life in a meaningful way, are you doing a good job

40

displaying that fact to them in a way that they *fully get it?* This time I will urge to you go to https://app.acuityscheduling.com/schedule.php?owner=18229448 and use the 15 minutes of free consultation to get a representative to give you some tips if you *need them.* This part is where I see businesses that **could** truly change the world go bankrupt, and ethical hard-working people, who try to take care of their family, lose everything, because they couldn't manage to communicate with their customers in a **meaningful and honest way**... If you think you are not at your true potential please *go to* https://app.acuityscheduling.com/schedule.php?owner=18229448 or call someone who is an expert in this and has the record to **prove it**, because I genuinely believe with all of my heart that no matter how much value you could add to the world, if you don't master this step you won't really go far...

Step 5: Excite

To some extent most businesses have the aforementioned techniques implemented in their business model, but since you stayed so far, I have some tricks that you can have up your sleeve that will raise your ARPU (Average Revenue Per User) by 15%-65%. So, what is it you ask? Well, it's very simple really. After a sale has occurred and the exchange of money for services/product has happened, then what? What do you do to keep you customers happy, and keep them? See, this is crucial if you want your business to be the best, because the game is not just getting new customers all the time, it's also keeping the ones you have happy. This is not just an ethical way to show **gratitude**, it is also very important for the flow of this journey from here to the next steps. Remember, *we go through every step to get to the next*, and we go through that process to increase the fuel of business so it can expand so the cycle can happen again. So ask yourself now, how can you keep the people who have made the bold and wise choice to exchange their precious money for whatever you're offering? Are there any free gifts that you can give to them that will keep you in their heart? Is there any crucial information that you can give to them related to your business that they would be interested in knowing? In what ways can you please them *without them even asking for it*? Now that's some brain food right there. An example of someone who did this in an impeccably marvelous way is the **formal education system**. Think about it, you go through 12 years of middle school and high school, then you move on to "higher education". There, you **spend tens of thousands of dollars per year** to get a diploma that more than 90% doesn't give you the credibility or the skill to go to the workforce, and they have the tenacity to *up-sell* you into an MBA or a master's degree. You see, they find ways to make it so necessary for your life that *you find yourself paying them for years and years to*

43

come... While this is not exactly popular opinion, it is certainly worth acknowledging the success of the formal education sector if we want to be able to model something similar in your business.

Step 6: Ascension

Now your customer has bought from you once and you're doing a good job keeping them happy. What's the next rational step that goes hand in hand the previous one? Have them buy another product of yours that will make their life even more full of joy now that they have already committed once to buying from you once. See more often than not as I mentioned a couple of steps earlier, **people buy from who they know.** Guess what, they not only know you by this point, but if your product is as good as we claimed it is (which it **needs to be**) then they also *trust you...* So, it would be *unethical not reaching out to them* when you think there is something more that can make their life better. Now, do you notice how all of the steps are coming together? While all of them isolated are good to get the job done, the more you stack on top of one-another the more **exponentially powerful** the formula becomes! Here are some questions again to help *guide you* towards where you are *headed towards*. Are there any supplementary products to the one they bought that can *cumulatively add value* to them? Can you potentially make another product just to come and supplement the one they bought right before? Are you making sure they don't forget your name? Oh, by the way speaking of remembering the name: **SKYLINE CONSULTING** https://app.acuityscheduling.com/schedule.php ?owner=18229448. You see, this right there would be a perfect example of making sure people remember you, but most businesses fail to do that because they don't truly believe their **service can offer tremendous value to**

people who are willing to use it! A final thought on this to keep your mind occupied would be to think of Amazon's purchase screen... Next time you're buying something from there, just take a quick look at the "people also bought" section... If Amazon does it, then it might be fairly smart to think about *doing it yourself.*

Step 7: Advocate/Promote/Partner

This is where we have been heading this whole time. Think of this not as the end of the journey but merely the transition from **one epoch to another**. Just like in life, we don't dance, sing, paint, travel *because we want to be over with it, we do it because every minute of it gives us unprecedented pleasure for no apparent reason other than we're there now.* Same way, your customer journey is not just something that leads to step 7 and then there is nothing; rather I would argue it is a graceful journey with a lot of transactions during the way that ultimately leads to the next phase of the cycle. You see, in this step you have to really think about how you can take the relatively small percentage of people who are with you up to this point and have them **actively promote** your brand. How cool would it be if you could see the progression of someone first meeting your brand and going through all the steps up to the point where *they are the ones telling others how awesome the empire you have built is!* Some questions that will again act as your point of reference when you are navigating through the final step would be the following. How do you **incentivize** people to spread the word and make other people aware of your product? Is there a reason beyond the product itself as to why they would want to be your advocate? How do you make sure these people are treated like **gold?** Have you figured out a step-by-step strategy that allows step 7 people to have the *most benefits?*

Now, there is another part to this journey

that very few people will manage to get there. That is **partnering** with you. I will give you a simple example. When creating **Skyline Consulting,** I wanted to make sure that whether I was around or not, our clients were given the *honor pledge* that we will not sleep, not eat, not drink until they **see the results they were promised.** To make sure there was a system that accurately represented my *vision of the company,* I reflected back to the 7 steps and I thought about no. 7 itself. See, what we ended up doing is we created a system that makes sure companies that *consult us* are given the most **intense care and utter commitment** so that one day we might be able to partner with them and get to truly share have a *stake in the game*, something most consultants at the thought of have their hearts filled with sheer terror. See, they want the upside without any downside; **they make money if you win, and they do too if you lose**.

We on the other hand, have every **incentive**

to make you successful, we don't care about quick and easy money, our mission is to truly get your business to its true potential. Everyone who works at **Skyline Consulting** knows for sure that we value your business more than anything, and we **will** go to insane lengths to **make that happen**. Please, don't take my word for it! Actually go https://app.acuityscheduling.com/schedule.php ?owner=18229448 and *schedule a call for the 15 minutes free advice* and pay attention to the unfathomable determination of the people who represent us. If two traits were able to sum up the **Skyline Consulting** mindset, which I highly advise you to adapt it in your organization's mentality, they would be: being able to have the **tenacity** to set outrageous goals and challenge the status quo if need be, while also having the **flexibility** to be willing to do anything that *gets you there*! https://app.acuityscheduling.com/schedule.php ?owner=18229448.

HOW TO MAKE YOUR BUSINESS #1 IN YOUR INDUSTRY
WITHIN 90 DAYS OR LESS

THE GRAND FINALE: "I PRAY FOR THE WISDOM TO DO THE RIGHT THING AND THE COURAGE AND PERSEVERANCE TO DO IT"

Now you have read your way to the very end of this booklet... You have gathered information that partly might have been known to you and information that might have been truly the begging of a *new era* in your business... Regardless, your decision to read this book is **invaluable**, since you acquired a true, solid conscious grasp of how you can make your organization great. I hope you shared my enthusiasm and passion throughout, but the most important step is: what now? See, *I kept the promise I gave* you in the beginning and I gave you small slices of a lot of information that if you take them and implement them in your organization after some period of trial and error and some change in the structure you will definitely be able to really improve your business. Now, it is clear that you can take the hard do-it-yourself approach and build upon the slices of *intelligence* that you read about in here or, and I really hate to say it, you can work with someone who knows not only the small bits and pieces of information, but also reads the grander picture while having the *experience* and *intelligence* to overcome obstacles that **will** take place. This way, your chances of actually achieving to get your business to lengths that you had not even imagined, increases by a tenfold if you *ask me*. The real reason though, lies in the fact that we are humans and we are wired to work in a certain way. You see, in order to achieve something, you need to be fully **committed** to achieving it. A successful man once said to one

of his mentees who was having an asthma
attack while swimming, grasping and begging
for fresh air... He said, "How bad do want to
get some fresh air?" as he vehemently held the
boy underwater. The boy couldn't even speak,
he was feeling the **powerlessness** of chocking
many people with asthma have felt before. He
was not giving up, though, he knew he had to
get out of there and *breathe*. A wrestler
overturning the other, stronger wrestler, the boy
managed to get out of the water and squeeze his
lungs, inhaling with all the power that was left
in his body and *soul,* just to get some fresh air.
After 5 minutes or so, when he finally adjusted,
exhausted he asked the man "Why did you do
that?". The man smiled, softly looked at him
with sparkling eyes, and said "In order for you
to succeed, **you have to want it as much as
you want to breath...**". The boy at that
moment glistened with an enlightening sense of
true comprehension of the thing he came to
seek from the mentor, his *help to succeed.* The boy

then hesitantly asked "So how do you actually get to achieve what you are saying?". The man again looked at the boy and with a voice that reverberated wisdom said "All you have to do is **commit**. The world is yours for the taking if you learn to **commit** your mind to your dreams and coordinate your actions in such a way that they get you one step closer at a time.". At that point the boy paused. He exclaimed to the man in a tone that made uncertainty vanish from the corners of the earth "The boy died a couple of minutes ago under the water. I am a man now, and I am all that's left." The guru smiled and gently said "You are ready, your journey has just begun. *We shall commence?*"

See the guru knew that in order for the boy to be able to take over the island, he needed to **burn the boats.** He needed to **commit** in what he believed in, in what he was *meant to do*. He was *destined* to succeed all he needs do is make the decision to **commit**. So, what do good commitments have in common? They all share

two, and only two traits. One is time. For one
to commit, he/she needs to devote a lot of time
in whatever it is they are trying to do. Time is
the part of the equation that's valuable, because
no matter what we do, we cannot get it back.
We can prolong our lives by *leading* a healthy
life, but we can never get back time that we lost.
**Time is arguably the most valuable asset we
have**, and if *you want to commit by now* you need to
invest it wisely. The second aspect to the
commitment equation is money. We can see
miracles in front of us and knowledge that
withstands the bonds of time, but we just might
miss it because it was there for everyone to see.
By now, you probably, *like me*, have seen or
heard something from someone that if you were
to go back *in time* and implement that change to
an aspect of your life or your business, you
would increase that aspect dramatically. I mean
think about it, advice that is free is just
conversation, whereas advice that you pay for is
immediately **more valuable**, because you paid

55

for it. However, the most important thing to me is that money is a *measure of exclusivity*. Now, I don't mean that in a bad way, I mean it in the sense that it is through exchanging money for a service/ product, you get to have the upper hand over the competition. Now, the *example* I'm using with advice is not to say that this principle doesn't apply to every sort of service or product, I just mention it because *I know it best*. So that principle applies to your business as well. Sometimes you will be faced with a choice of giving something in exchange for something 10, 20, 50, 1000 times greater that maybe *only you and a select group of people can see*. It is in your best interest to evaluate this investment not in how big of an "expense" you think it might be in the moment, but in terms of providing future **unprecedented** value. Key word being *unprecedented*. In something as investing unprecedented could be a return of 20% on your investment within a set timeframe after your *deal is done*. In something a little more complex, such as health, you expect unprecedented returns by doubling your BMI. Point is, whatever it is you're after, check the actual *price* you pay, that is how much value you're going to get out of it compared to the money you are going to *pay for it*.

Hopefully, this short guide gave an exclusive look into fragments of information about what makes a business great and what destroys entire empires... It was my pleasure and honor being your *guide* throughout this journey of exploration and learning, but the journey just *begin*s here. **You** are now responsible for figuring out ways to improve your business and your life, ways to innovate and create, and most importantly the *right people who will do all that stuff for you*. You see no matter how much I would like it for you to *jump on Skyline Consulting's website and make schedule an appointment*, I recognize that some people are going to find ways to do it their own way and I respect that. *Now*, if you choose to do that, please let me know what you found and how this book helped you *get there*. Again, I loved taking through this path and acting as *guiding light* to those who might need it most... If you ever feel you need professional insight from me and my team, go https://app.acuityscheduling.com/schedule.php?owner=18229448 and give me call.

Your Loyal friend,

Mike Pantouvakis

ABOUT THE AUTHOR

Mike Pantouvakis has acted as consultant for business in over 15 industries in more than 7 states and 3 countries. He attends one of the best business schools in the world, NYU Stern School of Business, yet he has a vast experience in business making. He started his fist venture at the age of 16, building one of the first successful Instagram advertising pages. Spending his summers working at financial institutions, advising deals, and creating models, he quickly developed a passion for scaling businesses through smart, ethical, and profitable practices. He has since learned to navigate the jungle of social media - after 5 years of rigorous experience - and has turned to helping other scale their dreams of being financially free. He now runs a consulting firm located in the heart of New

York City.